ಸಂ

"My experience with this book was not what I expected. Courtney's powerful story pulled me out of my sterile environment and thrust me into the nightmare in which her family and thousands of others live. That nightmare, being the incredibly challenging, sometimes horrifying, and unrelentingly stressful 24/7 life with an autistic child. She candidly relates her deepest feelings and experiences, most of them bad, from which there seems to be no escape. She reaches out of the pages, grabs her readers by the heart, and pulls them into her world. A world where they learn of tenacity and stubborn refusal to give up on behalf of an innocent child. It is a book that you don't really want to read, but is so compelling, you cannot put it down. It will forever change those of us on the outside of the autism environment, looking in, maybe playing a role in it, but having never really lived it. God bless you, Courtney, and your family"

-James D. Smith, DC, CCN, DACBN

COURTNEY RIEGEL

THROUGH A
MOTHER'S EYES

*a spiral down
       the autism spectrum*

TATE PUBLISHING & *Enterprises*

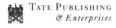 Tate Publishing
& Enterprises

Through A Mother's Eyes
Copyright © 2006 by Courtney Riegel. All rights reserved.

No part of this publication may be reproduced, stored in a retrieval system or transmitted in any way by any means, electronic, mechanical, photocopy, recording or otherwise without the prior permission of the author except as provided by USA copyright law.

The opinions expressed by the author are not necessarily those of Tate Publishing, LLC.

This book is designed to provide accurate and authoritative information with regard to the subject matter covered. This information is given with the understanding that neither the author nor Tate Publishing, LLC is engaged in rendering legal, professional advice. Since the details of your situation are fact dependent, you should additionally seek the services of a competent professional.

Book design copyright © 2006 by Tate Publishing, LLC. All rights reserved.
Cover design by Rusty Eldred
Interior design by Jennifer Redden

Published in the United States of America

ISBN: 1-5988659-0-0
06.09.01

Dedication

For Jared, Noah, and Abby– I Love You

Acknowledgments

A heartfelt thank you to author Karyn Seroussi, whose book entitled *Unraveling the Mystery of Autism and PDD*, got the ball rolling in helping my son. Her words were helpful, informative, and above all, inspiring.

I would also like to thank James Smith, D.C., and Anju Usman, M.D., who in the past and future play an important role in helping my son "wake up." To my family, who have always believed in the ideas I have had to help Noah. For both of my parents, who help make sure that finances aren't an issue when things get rough.

To Daniel, for working so hard for us.

For Addie, Tony, and Avery, for just being there. May God watch over us all.

Table of Contents

Introduction..................................11
Diaper Rash and Dreary Days..................15
The Twilight Zone............................23
The Black Shadow.............................29
Preschool Panic..............................35
My Mission...................................41
The Search...................................47
Nurse Hatchet's Staff........................55
Big Boy School...............................61
All of the Whoopla...........................67
Washington D.C...............................75
Diets, Detox, and Drugs…oh my!...............79
Set Nothing in Stone.........................87
Helpful Links................................

Introduction

Most books start off with the author introducing themselves with their degrees. Well, I am not a doctor, nor do I have a Ph.D. I do have a career diploma as a Paraprofessional for Special Education, and I am working on an Associate's degree in Early Childhood Education, but for this it seems irrelevant. When it comes down to it, my experiences as a parent rise above all. I was lucky enough to be able to have three children. One of my three is a special needs child. He has autism. This is an experience and an *education* I live and fight for everyday.

What I do know about autism I was forced to learn. I didn't have to hit it as hard as I did, but what kind of parent would I be if it wasn't my top priority? I opted to bring my children into the world. I can't sit by relaxed unless I feel I am doing all I can to make his life easier with the limitations that are thrown out to him. My purpose for being alive is to make an impression on him. I hope to give him enough strength to survive this world without me.

Please don't get me wrong. I am not claiming to be a martyr or some freak who found something spiritual in my meatloaf. I am *not* even close to being perfect. I have learned that an advocating, knowledgeable parent is a strong parent. I have changed the way I think about the world. The best advice I can offer other parents forced to digest this epidemic is to accept and move toward the future. We can't change the past. I can't go back and change the way certain things were handled with my son. I can't take back his vaccines or make it so he was diagnosed earlier to gain more recovery. What I can do is learn and move on. Try to turn every normal emotion that goes along with this into strength. Never be ashamed or apologetic of your child's behavior. Be a strong pair of eyes, ears, and a voice to advocate their needs. Stop trying to please everyone else. It doesn't matter if the school board thinks you are a pain in the butt, or if you get on the doctor's nerves. Get the answers you need so you can spend more time with your child and less time in emotional crisis.

I am obsessed with finding new knowledge to help my son. If writing this book helps just one family learn something new, I can rest assured that I "paid it forward." We know that no two children are alike, but if you walk away from this book inspired to at least try something new or have the desire to learn more, then his story was worth sharing.

My son, Noah, was born into my little part of the world for a reason. He is more than just an individual with autism. He is a son, a grandson, a great grandson, a cousin, a brother, a nephew, a friend, a teacher, and a joy to know. Above everything else, he is loved. Noah is and always will be my personal hero.

Signs and Symptoms of Autism

Usually, a child is diagnosed between the ages of eighteen months and three years old. Many parents claim that their children appeared "normal" (I hate that word) until receiving certain vaccines. Most claim the MMR (Mumps, Measles, and Rubella) vaccine did the damage. The severity of symptoms can vary from mild to severe.

<u>Signs can include but are not limited to:</u>
- A resistance to any cuddling or affection
- An obvious delay or lack of language
- No interest in surrounding objects (toys, people, etc.)
- Does not make eye contact
- Avoids responding to others
- Prefers to be alone
- Does not point to surroundings or ask, "What's that?"
- Over- or undersensitive to danger
- Failure to socialize or make friends
- Unable to understand nonverbal communication skills

- Neediness for routine
- Repetitive language
- Inappropriate social skills
- Abnormal playing
- Frequent outbursts and/or tantrums
- Delays in acquiring motor skills
- Appears to be deaf
- Abnormal sensory stimuli (loud noises, bright lights, smells, crowds, etc.)
- Self-stimulating behavior

Chapter One

Diaper Rash and Dreary Days

My life. I have found that over the years, my life is just the opposite of a family sitcom, or even a good cliché. Nothing, and I do mean nothing, in my home is or has been quiet and "calm as a mouse." However, I wasn't prepared for what would take place two years after my wedding.

Daniel and I were young when we were married. I started dating him my senior year in high school. Despite all of the odds not in our favor, being nineteen and twenty years old, we tied the knot.

Before the wedding, we decided to take adult Bible classes at a Christian church in our town. We both came from families who weren't real "church goers." I wanted to be accepted in that community, so we did all of the extra activities to be social. One lesson that stood out in my mind was that of being "tested." The comment about God testing you beyond all belief was made. Were we strong enough as a couple to handle this? An older couple was describing all of the "tests" at the beginning of their marriage. They were simple things, like apartment and job issues. We expected that. Needless to say, we got a little more.

Do you remember when people made the old statement, "I wouldn't wish that on my worst enemy!" as you grew up? Well, with some things you experience through life, I imagine that is in fact true. My biggest experience, the one that I couldn't even pass along to someone I disliked the most, would be autism. I am not embarrassed or ashamed of my son in any way. It is just so challenging and mysterious enough to drive one mad.

This is the experience that has forever changed my life. It has changed how I see the world and how I live in it. I will never be the same person I was before I had to ingest this lifestyle twenty-four hours a day. Unfortunately, millions of people will have to face this widely spread epidemic.

Autism. A short six-letter word that changes everything and everyone involved. Not only does the individual diagnosed have to face a tough road in life, but the parents suffer as well, especially the mothers of these children. That would be me. My name is Courtney, and I have three wonderful children. (Doesn't every mother think that of her own?) Jared, Noah, and Abby were happily welcomed into our lives. My husband and I started our life together younger than the average couple, but things seemed really good. We had a family and a nice home, what more could one want?

Let's go back about nine years. Our oldest son, Jared, was already born and entering his "terrible twos" (cue the scary music). Our second son, Noah, soon followed. He entered the world exactly one week before Christmas (a pretty good present, if you ask me). He was an adorable, chubby, bald baby! I was instantly in love. He was perfect.

Jared was too young to remember Noah's birth, but was excited to see the new Elmo doll we had waiting for him in my hospital suitcase. Over time, though, a bond would form stronger than I am sure he could ever imagine.

I was much more relaxed in the hospital with this birth. Noah seemed content from the minute he was born. I decided to forego nursing; it just wasn't for me. Everything about nursing worried me. When the time came for me to feed Noah, I asked the staff to bring me soy formula.

Jared had colic his first few weeks of life (not a good thing when you start off in a small apartment building). The doctors ended up switching him to soy before it ended.

My hopes were to avoid that with Noah by just *starting* him out on soy. He took his first bottle with ease. All seemed perfect. He reminded me so much of Jared as a baby, which wasn't too long ago. Noah was a typical newborn. He slept a lot, made little squeaky noises, and grasped our fingers tightly in his first few hours of life, unaware of the flashing camera addiction his Aunt Stephanie had.

We waited for that first *typical* black stool and changed him several times. Poop. It isn't the nicest word or thought, but hey… it happens! I just never imagined it would end up being such a big deal later on.

Once we got home, things started to fall into place.

Surprisingly, Jared wasn't too jealous of his new brother. Noah settled in fine the first couple of days, but was rushed to the Emergency Room on Christmas Day when his circumcision became infected. Besides that drama, he was sleeping well at night and sucking his bottles down quickly. He burped very well, so I wasn't worried about him exploding. We were living our life like a normal family, and then we hit our first brick wall.

Noah's diaper changes started to become more frequent, and then never really stopped. He had a bowel movement three or four times an hour. They were so messy and grainy in texture. It would just flow out of him like water. At this point, he screamed each time a baby wipe or washcloth touched him. I began to bring bowls of warm water into his room and pat him clean. The phone calls to our doctor started. I was usually crying on the phone while explaining *loudly* that my newborn baby was losing layers of his skin due to diaper rash, and nothing was working to heal him! He was literally exploding with diarrhea, and even using yeast infection cream under the diaper rash ointment (like they suggested) made him worse. Seeing him in pain as I held him, so tiny in my arms, was making me sick.

Finally, after many phone calls to the doctor's office, I got the appointment that gave me a little bit of an answer. The doctor told me that it "looked like Rotavirus." He didn't say it *was* Rotavirus, but he said it *looked* like Rotavirus.

Being a young mother, I accepted a *maybe* answer and went home with directions to add rice cereal to his bottles. (Rice cereal=healthy bottom?)

As of today, I now know a little bit more about what

it actually is. Apparently, it is a common virus often found in children. It looks like a wheel when viewed under a microscope and can last 10+ days. Many symptoms follow this, including: severe diarrhea, watery stool, cramping, and raw skin. There have also been reports of death. It can be contagious, too, but nobody else in the house had any flu-like symptoms. We aren't really sure how he got the virus, unless it came home with him from the hospital. We even avoided Christmas calling to avoid germs. How ironic. The cereal did help his stool slow down and start to form better, which in turn helped his raw skin. I literally kept three to five layers of ointment under his diaper at all times, just in case. The cereal fattened him up quickly, and we use to joke that he would be a football player or a bouncer! If only I had purchased stock in Pampers. Our lives went back to *normal*, along with Noah's poop. For a little bit, that is.

  The days passed and slowly turned to months. Noah was developing perfectly. He cooed and blabbered right on target. He was always making those wet raspberry noises and getting everyone soaked. He was reaching each milestone asked for by his baby book that I scribbled in occasionally. Noah was really starting to interact with his family. He adored his Mickey Mouse bouncy seat (giving me a heart attack when he flipped himself over), and then slowly moved on to a walker, where he would watch his brother and scream at the dog. I loved watching him roll over and drag his body across the rug (you know, that "army guy under barbed wire" movement). None of my kids really crawled. He was making wonderful eye contact and clapping his tiny hands to all of his musical books and toys. At eleven months, he pulled himself up and took his first steps… turning and smiling at us with that little gap between his front teeth. He began to say a few words, like "dada" and "momma," and other things I am sure aliens could have made out. He loved to be rocked to sleep on my lap and cuddle with his Elmo doll. Jared was at preschool a couple mornings a week, so Noah kept me busy, dragging his basket of toys everywhere. I have all of those wonderful memories of his infant years in my scrapbooks and in my heart. My son, Noah Joseph, was sent to me from Heaven as a healthy, intelligent, *normal* baby boy. A mother knows these things.

They say parents are a little more at ease with their second child. I would have to agree with that, at least in the beginning of things. Things seemed to be fine in our home. I missed my husband because he worked all the time, and he missed out on a lot of things with the boys. It was important to us that they didn't grow up in daycare or with a sitter. I was very happy with my boys. Perhaps a little too happy, because I didn't notice that a monster was lurking in the shadows of our lives.

Noah was getting close to the age of fifteen months, and it was time for another well baby checkup. I knew he would be getting his MMR vaccine, so I gave him Tylenol before we left. His examination went fine, and he was right on target developmentally. He started to run a fever not too long after his vaccine.

It was a nasty day as far as the weather was concerned. The dreary sky made a perfect excuse to take a nap under a warm quilt. That is exactly what Noah did when we returned home. I remember checking on him throughout the day. I thought he was sleeping really well because of the dark sky, but it wasn't the rain making him sleep. His vaccine was making him sleep. It was poisoning him, affecting his brain and tiny body. When my baby woke up that afternoon, he was gone. My beautiful boy lost himself in his *own* body.

Chapter Two

The Twilight Zone

    I have a television that runs nonstop reruns of movies and useless television programs in my head. It is ridiculous for someone to watch something once and be able to remember the lines and quote them for the rest of their lives. Rod Sterling visits me a lot. That deep voice telling me things are no longer what they seem. I believe him too. I have witnessed the sudden changes in my house. We never got a warning, like those waiting out a bad storm. We were just hit head-on with something that we couldn't explain. Our whole world changed in the blink of an eye…that huge Twilight Zone eye at the beginning of each episode. I desperately needed the channel changed.

    As the weeks went on after Noah's last checkup, I noticed a lot of differences in him. His entire character had changed. He was irritable at times, and lifeless at others. His cry even changed. It was so high-pitched it was almost unbearable. The simple words he could express changed to low grunts and eventually temper tantrums, for I could no longer understand his needs or make him happy. He lost himself in his toys or cartoons. Noah never made eye contact with any of us and never turned his head when we spoke to him. As far as he was concerned, we didn't exist. The whole situation was frustrating.

Being as concerned as I was, I took Noah to the doctor a few more times for answers. At this point, I was told a lot of things, such as "boys talk later," or "I'm sure his language is there, but sometimes older siblings answer for them." No one really explained why the language he did have had stopped.

Noah was still napping well and eating fine. He really took to his milk now, drinking many cups a day. His eyes turned hazy and spaced out, while his cheeks had a constant rosy glow. I look back at photos now and can see that his stomach was extended and bloated.

One day, I walked into his bedroom where he was staring out his window. I talked to him and he looked up. Our eyes never met, but he seemed to be looking my way. The only problem was he didn't care who I was. It was almost as if he could see right through my soul.

I felt very anxious and entertained an old friend of the past…an anxiety attack.

A dark shadow seemed to be dwelling over us, but I couldn't catch it long enough to see what it was. I felt like a failure as a mother and my marriage suffered. Some of the things in my life I was once concerned about no longer existed. Daniel and I fought as his work hours increased, and I had to face all of the changes with Noah alone. His work literally took everything he was able to give. I stood there alone, looking down a long hallway that kept getting longer.

Jared was noticing a change in his brother, too, as he was ignored when trying to interact. Noah didn't seem to play appropriately with his toys. He didn't have that creative imagination like his brother did at his age. He didn't know *how* to play.

He was suffering from more ear infections, and we started seeing a new doctor concerning his in toeing. He fell over everything as he got bigger. His feet literally turned in to the point that the tips of his toes touched. Dan and I really didn't know if Noah was going to need some sort of brace from the knee down to help correct his legs. The doctor took X-rays, and really felt that they would correct themselves as he grew taller over the years. The muscles in his legs would stretch as he gained height, pulling his feet straighter. On top of everything else, Noah was constantly getting hurt because he tripped while walking. He never cried, though. In fact, he liked to hurt himself in many ways. It was as if he enjoyed pinching his skin or banging his head into things. I was on call all day to make sure Noah wasn't injuring himself.

One afternoon, Dan and I decided to send the boys to my parents' house. My chest had been bothering me, and we both decided that a break from the ordinary routine would do us good. We went out for lunch and caught a movie. When returning, we noticed that my mother had this *look* on her face. Immediately, my parents started in on us about their concerns with Noah. "Look," my mom said as she clapped her hands behind Noah's head as he looked at his blocks on the floor. "We think he is deaf," she told me while glancing at my dad. Maybe it was shock or maybe it was anger, but in any case, I couldn't respond. Hot tears formed, but I refused to let them run down my face. How could they think I was that stupid? Daniel and I knew something was going on. We wanted answers. I just didn't want to vocalize my fears to the world. It made me physically ill to talk about the things Noah was or wasn't doing, and just *how* different he really was from Jared at his age. We got the boys in the car and left. My feelings were hurt, and I hated the world. I hated my life. How I wanted to wreck the car and remove us all from this pain. The truth is hard to face, even if you already are aware of it.

The stress and unanswered questions continued each day. We ran away from it all one week over the summer. Being a parent was the hardest thing in the world in our shoes, even at Disney World. The temper tantrums were constant. Noah freaked out on several occasions, mostly due to the crowds. Looking at other parents who were dealing with typical tantrums because their child wanted every toy in the gift shop made me jealous. It was a very long vacation. We ended up spending extra time visiting Dan's sister while we were out of state. He screamed the entire visit. I guess it is true when they say you can never really run away from your problems. I guess all of the excitement and restaurant food had finally taken its toll on Noah. He broke out in a strange rash all the way home. Daniel and I exchanged glances in the car. We both knew that we needed a vacation from this vacation, but by *ourselves*.

Over those days following the trip, Dan and I both tried different things with Noah. Neither of us could get his attention when standing behind him making noise. "He isn't turning his head to look at us," I would scream in panic. Noah didn't seem affected by our emotional crisis.

He sat at dinner, happily sucking down spaghetti noodles as the world caved in all around us.

When Christmas time came around, we went to visit some of Daniel's family. Noah had just turned two years old. I love the holidays. The decorations, food, and lights make it is the best, however, I will never forget this particular visit. What happened that day hurt me. I didn't fall on an icy doorstep or hit the holiday "punch" too hard. It was nothing more than words. Words deep enough to cut skin.

One of Dan's brothers was playing around with all the little kids. He was trying everything to get Noah involved, but Noah wanted to be by himself. I heard him say his name a couple of times, and then across the house I heard him yell out, "What is with this kid? Is he deaf or something?" My heart skipped a beat and the tightening in my chest started back up. At this point in my life, a bullet might have been easier to take (ignorance and beer, always a good combo). I cried all the way home. Daniel and I fought yet again. I hated the world.

I made an appointment when Christmas was over to speak to the pediatrician again. Enough time had passed that we knew Jared wasn't *talking* for Noah. Noah was just different. He seemed miserable. I took him kicking and screaming into the doctor's office. I was trying hard to act like I wasn't being stared at. I was getting good at pretending that old, crabby couples weren't mumbling about us and how he needed a spanking. Of course it would end up being one of those times when you wait over an hour in the outside waiting room and another inside. The panic I was facing was really wearing me down inside. I felt old. I just wanted to sleep and forget everything.

Once inside the exam room, I demanded them to do something with Noah. I was sick of all of the excuses for why his language had stopped and why his personality had changed. We wanted to see a specialist! We wanted his hearing checked! They needed to call someone…they needed to just do something besides send me back home!

That something was a hearing test preformed at the hospital. Since Noah couldn't speak and tell us if he was hearing beeps like some tests, they were going to perform a Brainstem Evoked Response Test. This is used a lot with young infants. It measures the function of the brainstem in response to sounds. The results can provide information regarding hearing sensitivity, and can also let you know if the brainstem transmits noises the way it should.

They gave Noah a mild sedative in a drink to make him drowsy. This was to prevent him from pulling any wires off. We waited and waited, but it seemed to make him more hyper. He was really bouncing off the walls. The nurses left the room so we could try to rock him, but it didn't work. We had to let them give him a form of anesthetic. As I sat next to my son, watching him space out, I cried. He looked so helpless lying there as his eyes dilated. His face was red and blotchy from crying so much. He was sweating from hitting himself. I looked over at Daniel and thought about our future. We needed answers. We needed to know what took our son away from us that rainy afternoon in March.

Chapter Three

THE BLACK SHADOW

Did you ever run across your bedroom as a child, leaping half way onto the bed so the monster underneath couldn't touch your feet? As you grow up, most get the idea in their mind of being invincible. At least that is how I felt. Nothing bad would happen to me. I did my part in the community. I worked in a nursing home and helped people. I was safe. Evil, however, takes on many forms. At the ripe old age of twenty-four, I was dealing with a faceless monster, one that did make it out from underneath my son's bed. No amount of nightlights or lullabies on the Playskool radio could change that.

I should have felt relief when the phone rang a few days later, telling me Noah's hearing tests were fine. He could hear perfectly, in fact. I was glad, but more frustrated than anything. Again we sat in the doctor's office. This time, we were being sent to a children's neurologist. I took Noah back home and tried to handle life the best way that I could while waiting that long month they have you wait as a new patient. We stayed inside a lot, limiting our sunlight to the small patch of grass out back.

On the morning of the appointment, I stuck Noah in the tub and washed and dressed him. He had just a touch of blonde hair, and I smoothed it down. Nothing bad could happen to an adorable, chubby little boy in overalls, *right*? Wrong. The doctor came in and asked us a million questions as he watched Noah playing with the farm on the floor. He sat on the floor, trying to interact with Noah. Noah hated the small room, and after awhile, he started to scream. Dan picked him up to comfort him, giving him the perfect opportunity to reach the light switch. He began to flip it on and off, giving the room a strobe light effect. I apologized while we were talking, and explained how Noah is often calmed by repeating things (opening and closing cabinets and doors, lights on and off). He nodded in agreement. I wanted to throw up. I felt very defensive all of a sudden. I shouldn't apologize for a two-year-old who obviously was having issues, should I?

The room seemed to have stopped for those few short seconds it took for the doctor to finally open up his mouth and say something. "I know what's going on with your son," he started to say. I gulped. My stomach was in my throat. *What does that mean?* I wondered to myself, *Oh no, he found something wrong.* I looked down at the ugly carpet in his office.

He went on to tell us that he has seen this many times before and blah, blah, blah, something or other, and I heard the words "Autism Disorder." The movies, all of those darn *Lifetime* movies I have seen about this went buzzing through my head. Daniel asked what that meant, and I screamed, "Rain Man!" I bent over my chair and sobbed. I cried hard and loud like a kid who fell off his bike and skinned *both* knees. I missed some of the conversation because the room seemed to have moved. That awful carpet was mocking me.

The doctor was describing Noah as falling under the PDD-NOS category (Pervasive Developmental Disorder-Not Otherwise Specified). Now, as I sit and write this, I know it still means autism. It is just lower on the autism spectrum. It is a made-up medical term to comfort hysterical parents until they can learn to say the "A" word.

He wanted us to call and get a little help through the State for Noah since he was still under the age of three. We paid and made our next appointment. Imagine paying someone to tell you that your child's life is doomed. The dark shadow was now captured. It had a face and a name. This made it more personal. In the movies, you know that garlic frightens a vampire and silver kills a werewolf, but this monster didn't have a weapon or cure. This wasn't a movie; this was my son's life. This was *our* life.

We rode home in silence.

I truly believe that parents grieve for the loss of a child diagnosed with a lifetime disability just as much as those who have lost a child in death. All of the images you had of your children, your hopes for who they would be and what they would do in the world, die. An image like this is hard to give up. Jared and Noah are twenty months apart. I had images of them being in high school together, playing sports, and calling girls. Thoughts of college, marriage, and even grandchildren from both of them, a *normal* life.

After grief comes anger. Not just anger, but a pure

hatred for anyone else who had children. I would see parents out walking with their kids, looking so content. I wanted to run them over, back up, and run them over again. I was depressed. You know the woman you see in the grocery store who has six kids all under the age of ten? She is yelling at every one of them for walking too slow or blinking too much. You know her. Every town has one. All of *her* kids are healthy. I hated her for that. I didn't smoke or do drugs, and I rarely had a drink. I even gave up caffeine during my pregnancy. I took my prenatal vitamins, saw the doctor, and took care of myself. Why me? Why my child? He wasn't a mistake or result of a one-night stand. He was wanted. The worst thing I can think of was eating cookie dough while baking one day. According to my eighty-three-year-old grandma, you will "get worms," not autism. Nothing made sense anymore, and nothing was fair.

The stress between Daniel and me kept brewing. I remember telling his friends to stop coming over to our house. I even acted rude enough to keep them away. I just couldn't handle the stupid stories about their immature lives anymore. I hated them for being able to make Dan laugh. He wasn't allowed to laugh as far as I was concerned. I didn't want laughter in the house. I wanted to be miserable and robotic.

The only thing we had to look forward to was the upcoming help Noah was suppose to receive from the State. I really wanted to meet someone who worked with other children with delays. This wasn't going to be an easy process. It took us over two months to get the paperwork done, and finally, someone called. She was coming to my house to meet Noah. She was going to start speech therapy through play. Everything was set up, but the day came and went. She didn't show up. I kicked a hole in the hallway wall. I told Daniel I fell.

Eventually, Noah did receive a couple of months of therapy, but it was a real mess. We went through three different girls in that short time. One would quit or get transferred; one was abducted by a UFO or something. It was awful.

After his third birthday, it was up to the School District to help him. I was glad, but nervous. The previous so-called help made me leery. Perhaps we could accomplish something now. He had waited long enough. We all had waited long enough.

Daniel and I decided to take a trip to Indiana to visit my sister and her husband. It would be good for us to take a break (obviously we forgot about Florida when making these plans). Jared was a pain on the car ride, but Noah did wonderfully. Things seemed great.

We decided to take the boys to see a movie that night. Noah had only been to the show once before. Unfortunately, five minutes into Shrek, he decided to freak out and jump out of his seat and throw a fit. Daniel took him back to my sister's house. I felt really bad about everything, and hated the fact that he was going to miss out on such a cute show. I could hear people whispering about us, and that was upsetting.

The next afternoon, we decided to go the Children's Museum (another brilliant idea). As we took a break for lunch, Noah started to scream in the food court. He didn't want to stop moving and wait in line. He threw himself down and started to scream. Tears were already filling my eyes. One particular family stopped dead in their tracks to stare. "Stop looking at us!" I cried. My sister walked up to them very calmly and informed them he had autism, and we were going through enough without them upsetting us by staring. It had to have embarrassed them. I'm sure they didn't realize how rude they were being. People are curious, but it is rude to stop what you are doing and stare. Guess what? The parents *do* realize what's going on in public with their child.

We left to go back home the next morning. It was obvious that we couldn't relax until more questions and solutions were figured out. So, what do overly stressed out couples do on a long car ride? They fight with each *other*, of course.

Chapter Four

Preschool Panic

We had to meet with a school psychologist and a member of the Special Education Department before Noah could qualify for the Special Needs Preschool program provided through our district.

They were very pleasant. The woman from the school was very nice, motherly, and soft-spoken. It made me feel comfortable about what was happening, and of course, Daniel was working, so I was doing this alone. I never once felt like I needed to explain Noah's behavior or lack of interest. I had to fill out a lot of paperwork while they tested him with toys, puzzles, flashcards, etc. Both seemed rather pleased at Noah's ability to sort and match objects, put puzzles together, and stack blocks. He did, however, continue to ignore every question they asked him. Agreeing that he did show delays cognitively, we set up his schooling. My anxiety attacks started back up. It dawned on me later that I would actually have to leave him there alone.

So there we were a few weeks later, standing in the hallway of the school. Other children were there waiting with their parents. I watched them and wondered if any of them had the "A" word. Noah was having a hard time standing still, and I felt my face get hot. Leaving him was torture. He ran after me crying and screaming. They told me it would be okay and shut the door. I sobbed. I kept reminding myself it was only three and a half hours. I heard him screaming once outside the building. I sat in the parking lot until I was able to stop crying and drive away. I was sick, but I did it. I hated Daniel for not being there, but this was my job. I was the parent that would stay home.

He started going to school very close to the end of the year. He never really bonded with anyone in that short time. They weren't able to really work with him. A few times when I would pick him up, he would be lying on the floor or on a beanbag chair, exhausted from crying. Sometimes, he would have the remains of vomit on his shirt from getting so upset. He was going through the same panic I was.

When school was out, I devoted my entire life to giving Noah homemade therapies. We purchased and were given many different educational toys and flashcards used in special education. Jared was eager to help out too. At night, I would be filled with conversations to throw at Dan about the things Noah did, or cry because it was so difficult getting him to sit down. I was constantly getting in Noah's face, forcing him to look at me. He scratched, slapped, kicked, and spit on me during tantrums. I tried to ignore this. I was adamant to continue this new mission. I wanted him better. "Look at me, Noah, what's this?

Where does the blue bear go?" Eventually, he understood that Mom wasn't going anywhere.

So we put puzzles together, put beads through a string, looked at lift-a-flap books, separated objects by sizes and colors, did matching pictures, and sang songs. He also received speech therapy in our home twice a week during the summer. The speech therapist was wonderful with Noah. He sat still for her and semi-paid attention. She always had a bag filled with musical toys and books. We didn't get a lot of language from him, but he was focusing better. I was thrilled! Even for that brief forty-five minutes, we had Noah and the monster didn't. If I was really lucky that day, Noah's hazel eyes would meet my hazel eyes for a split second before staring out, lost again.

When school started back up, we were greeted by a new paraprofessional (aide) that would be shadowing Noah while he was at school. She was there to keep him calm and focused while assisting him with academics when needed. It took me a couple weeks to start to relax. All of the therapists and aides in the past didn't last. Once I got used to the idea that she was there for the year, it was easier.

Noah didn't have a lot of communication abilities when he first started preschool. One thing his new paraprofessional suggested during his IEP meeting was the use of a system called PECS (Picture Exchange Communication System). They can be purchased online if needed, but I was lucky enough to borrow one from the school.

We kept a notebook of tiny cards that were full of language. For example, one card had a picture of a toothbrush. If Noah or I wanted his teeth brushed, we got out the card and handed it to each other. The card would have a drawing of a toothbrush on it, along with the word. Each card had Velcro on the back so it would stick inside the book safely. He seemed to enjoy using this system. I took every advantage to repeat words to him. The screams and grunts became less and less. He was now able to bring me a card of what he actually wanted. He took his book back and forth to school. This was also a wonderful way for the teachers to help express language to him. Simply showing him the recess card was so much easier for Noah to understand upcoming transitions.

After a short time, we worked on language building by adding the *wants* and *needs* cards. For instance, "I want pretzels," or "I need water." As time passed, he was slowly able to wean from the book. It was a wonderful experience that helped him communicate with us after the MMR vaccine took his ability away. This system was a very positive part of language building for Noah. The visual aides helped us all understand some of his needs.

With Jared off to elementary school, I had a couple of hours to myself. I dedicated that time to reading and researching. The laundry and dishes could wait. That should be crossed-stitched on a pillow.

I was getting really good at surfing the internet, so I sat down and went to work. I typed in "autism," and literally thousands of links came up. I just started at the beginning. I read and cried, and read some more. I went on a popular website that sells books and ordered a few to start out with. I am glad I did. This is truly what started the ball rolling.

I began with a book about a mother whose son was diagnosed with autism and the struggles she went through to get him better. Although there is not a cure for this disorder, there are so many things you could try to make things easier for them. Some parents have even stated that doctors undiagnosed their children as being Autistic. You start by doing simple things (so they say), like changing a diet or taking supplements. She also went on to explain the different therapies that had helped her son, and where they stood now on the spectrum. I finished her book in one day. I cannot explain it any better than this: I knew it would work for me too. I called Dan at work and explained what I was going to do. He agreed to give it a try. He knows me, though, and nothing was going to change my mind. We would try it for three months. I went to my parents and told them what I was going to do. I really needed some support. I went back home and made a list of everything she did with her son and where she got the items. This was my little list of hope. I knew I had a lot more research to do, but it was a start. I had a plan and that made me smile.

Chapter Five

My Mission

I curled up on the couch with my new list. How would I ever change his diet to gluten and casein free, get him on supplements, start all of his allergy and bowel testing, find a doctor, learn to shop and cook these strange foods, continue to research, continue his homemade therapy, take him to his school-assigned therapies, and take care of both boys and the house? I looked at the laundry piled to the ceiling and sighed.

The first thing I needed to try was changing Noah's diet. I had never heard of gluten or casein before, but they needed to be removed from his meals. Gluten is found in almost every food on the market. It is in wheat, oats, rye, barley, food additives, basically everything a person consumes daily. Casein is found in dairy products. It is the principal protein found in cow's milk. It is added to cheese, sherbet, yogurt, etc. On some manufacturer labels it can be called "caseinate," which I am told is the salt form of casein. In many Autistic people, gluten and casein act like opiates throughout the bloodstream. Their digestive systems cannot properly break down the proteins in these foods. The remaining peptides travel throughout the bloodstream and act like morphine in the functioning of the brain. If you take away these foods, the person will have withdrawal symptoms like a true drug user. Once the poisons leave the body, you will notice improvements in different areas, like speech and behavior. Gluten and casein sensitivities will not necessarily show up on a food allergy test either. It isn't an allergy, but more an inability to digest them. I am allergic to penicillin, so naturally when I think of an allergy, I picture hives or someone gasping for air.

The more I read and spoke with people who suffered these sensitivities, the more it amazed me. I kept finding research that claimed to improve the lives of people with things as simple as headaches and fatigue to more serious issues like depression, schizophrenia, and autism.

I wanted to have Noah tested for food allergies, as well as eliminate gluten and casein. I began to think about some of his favorite things to eat. You crave the foods that make you "high," or do the most damage. In order to get your next "fix," you have to eat them, which might explain Noah's love of milk. He loved cereal, pastas, orange juice, chicken nuggets, and milk.

I looked around my kitchen and thought about how difficult this would be. I began to clear out a shelf in the pantry *just for him*. I threw a lot of food away. I applied for another credit card and went to an organic market to start the shopping. I purchased rice-based pastas, gluten free/casein free waffles, organic peanut butter, spices, and meat that I knew didn't contain fillers. I was thrilled to find rice based non-dairy ice cream. I ordered potato based milk, tapioca breads, rice cereals, and crackers from the internet. I made sure we had plenty of fresh fruit and rice in our house. We even signed up for Culligan filtered water.

Something else to look for when eliminating foods is to monitor your child for a reaction to high phenol foods. These include apples, grapes, bananas, tomatoes, cocoa, oranges, and peanuts. A phenol is a chemical in food. A high buildup in the body can affect behavior and physical conditions. Some signs that your child might be having troubles with phenols are reddening in the ears and face, dark circles under the eyes, self-injuries, aggression toward others, and hyperactivity. There is a lot of information about phenols on the internet, along with the famous Feingold Diet.

The dreadful time came for Noah to eat. I made him some cereal. He took a bite and spit it back out. He was screaming and crying and on the floor in a tantrum. This went on for three days straight. Water was the only thing I could get down him. I began to question this diet, and my role as a parent. I looked to Daniel for answers, but he didn't know what to do either. Then it was as if fate stepped in. Noah accepted one-fourth of his organic peanut butter sandwich. We were thrilled! His growling tummy defeated the monster. I was able to breathe a little sigh of relief. At least for the moment.

Over the next few days, things got bad...really, really bad! Noah wasn't sleeping anymore, so I wasn't either. He yelled in pain, but where it hurt I couldn't tell you. I had to watch him roll around on the carpet, bang his head on the wall, rip at his hair, and kick the doors and cabinets. He sat on the toilet and punched himself in the stomach with the pain of constipation and threw up everywhere. He had a spaced out look to his face, black circles under his eyes, and bright red ears, all from the lack of gluten and casein. He looked and acted like he was dying. How frightening it was to watch! He looked so helpless. I wanted to give up and just grab him and hold him tightly to me. If I gave him a cup of milk, would he stop the self-destruction? I couldn't, or wouldn't, maybe both. I had to wait and see what was going to happen. My heart pounded as we waited it out.

Noah woke up from a long nap as if nothing had happened. His eyes were less glassy and dilated. He smiled at me. I held him very close and he didn't push me away. He let me give him a bath and make him some toast in his own toaster (even crumbs could contaminate). His tummy stood out, hard as a rock. It looked like it really hurt.

I remember hearing him laugh at a cartoon. I kept telling myself this was going to work, as I was constantly being reminded that autism had no cure.

When going back to preschool, Noah was hard to manage. His behavior spiked up and down over the next few weeks. He was on strict orders about his diet. He could only have what was brought from home. There was never to be an exception to this. They had to watch him closely so he wouldn't try to eat glue or paper. I even went as far as to send in homemade rice play-doh for him.

Time passed, and Daniel and I were excited to go back to the neurologist. Noah had started to say simple words, follow simple commands, and stay focused longer. He still had a lot of tantrums and behavior issues, but they seemed more spaced out. He still wouldn't potty train at the age of three and a half, but generally, he was looking better. All in all, it was going to be a great visit. We wanted to show off Noah's accomplishments over the last six months.

We were wrong. The doctor wasn't too impressed with all of the improvements. He rolled his eyes when I mentioned the diet, trying to make me feel ridiculous. He wasn't encouraging. He wouldn't sign any of the permission slips I needed to have some of the blood and stool work done that we were reading about. He didn't want to try anything for yeast buildup, or even have his food allergies tested. It was awful. The whole experience was disappointing. His attitude was of someone whose time was being wasted. Imagine parents who actually think alternative things *might* work! We walked out, but not before letting him know that "we would no longer need to see him."

A week later, we got a letter in the mail from his office, stating that if we needed his services, just to call for an appointment. I cussed him as I threw the letter in the trash. I had enough negativity going on. I know that I don't have a medical degree, but this seemed like common sense. It was obvious this diet was working on Noah. It was at least the start of something positive. When you are shown a little bit of faith, you don't just throw up your hands and give up. If our own doctor couldn't see that, we didn't need him. We were just going to find someone else. Unfortunately, as I was about to discover, that wasn't going to be easy. Then again, what about autism is easy? The school called. Noah was eating paper.

Chapter Six

The Search

I was reading online about different organizations that hold autism conferences. I wanted to meet other people and get some great advice. I read about a symposium not too far from us the next month and signed us up. In the meantime, Noah was four and progressing in school and at home. He was slowly building better vocabulary and showing different interests, like reading and working on the computer. He enjoyed speech and occupational therapy, and seeing his friends each day. It was wonderful to be able to hug him and have him respond. It was also great to see normal and appropriate crying. Before, he was immune to pain. He still wasn't interested in potty training. Once in a while, he would urinate in the potty. He was also getting used to being on his diet. Before, he used to try to sneak food. On Halloween, he had gotten a hold of an extra piece of hot dog bun and had a terrible reaction. He screamed and punched himself in the face and stomach. This lasted for four days. He had been clean and sober for so long, and then *bam*! The first signs of wheat hit him like a ton of bricks. His behavior carried on for a good two weeks after that episode. Thoughts of choking the neurologist went through my head. I knew it might take years to get him a lot better, but it would be worth it in the end. Those difficult days proved to us yet again that this diet *was* working on Noah.

The day of the symposium was very exciting. My stomach was hurting, but I assumed it was just nerves. Daniel and I attended as many lectures as we could. We bought more books and educational toys. We made sure to hit every booth set up and took every pamphlet we could carry. Some of the authors of books that I had read were there to speak, along with many doctors specializing in autism. We paid attention and took lots of notes. It was terrifying to hear about the number of people who had a child that was developing fine until they got their MMR vaccines. Mercury (not the planet, obviously) was making my son and thousands upon thousands like him turn Autistic. Mercury can cause neurotoxicity in people, especially infants, since their brains are still developing. This is when the exposure to natural or man made toxins alter the nervous system. Neurotoxicants can eventually kill neurons (the key signaling cells) in the brain. Thimerosal, a mercury compound, was added to vaccines starting in the 1930s. The first descriptions of autism came out in the 1940s. The children they were describing were born in the 1930s. According to the National Vaccine Information Center, it is estimated that today one in every one hundred fifty children born will be on the autism spectrum. This is an outrageous epidemic, and yet we still have those in the medical profession that deny any links.

As we walked our chubby little toddlers into the doctor's office for a routine checkup and vaccine, we were playing Russian roulette. Who would the poison be too much for, and who would be able to detox it?

Today, they claim vaccines to be thimerosal free. Many mercury-filled vaccines still linger on some doctors' shelves, as well as the flu vaccine, which also contains thimerosal.

We all know that vaccines are what doctors and most of society expect us to do with our children. As a parent, you hold the responsibility of becoming educated about both the benefits and risks of shots. This way, you can make the most informed decision for your child. Never, under any circumstance, have your child vaccinated if you have any doubts.

VACCINE INFORMATION

- Did you know that it is against the law for a doctor to give a vaccine without providing you with informational reading material prior to the shot?
- The majority of people just *assume* vaccines are safe.
- You should never give vaccines to sick children, even if it is only a sniffle.
- Vaccines can be separated and given at different times
- Thimerosal, a preservative added in the final part of a vaccine, can be toxic.
- Many vaccines exceed the safe level of mer-

cury. Some vaccines have included ingredients like formaldehyde, aluminum, chicken serum, MSG, monkey kidneys, sheep cells, eggs, antibiotics, fecal matter, pus from sores of diseased animals, and aborted human tissues.

- Did you know that you could say, "Not today, I want to take this home and read and research it first."

When it was time for Noah to start school, they asked me why he didn't finish his older toddler shots. I claimed it to be a religious belief. They cannot argue that. Remember, parents are in charge. Let a doctor talk until he is blue in the face if you are undecided or against vaccines.

I was starting to feel a connection with many of the presenters. They spoke of candida yeast in the gut, the gluten and casein free diet, speech therapy, ABA (Applied Behavioral Analysis), constipation, diarrhea, and vitamin supplements. We also learned about the Leaky Gut Syndrome, which was new to us.

We had the privilege of hearing high-functioning Autistic people speak as well. That really opened our eyes to some of the things we had or had not considered doing with Noah.

I again felt overwhelmed when we returned home with our huge notebooks of things to research. The first thing I wanted to do was find what they were calling a DAN (Defeat Autism Now) doctor. That should be an easy enough name for me to remember. A list of DAN doctors are listed on the internet by state. My state had two! How would I ever choose? I sighed as I phoned the first name on the list, only to find out minutes later he was retiring due to illness. I dialed the second number and got an appointment. The doctor was a chiropractor who was clinically trained in nutrition. We spoke, and I learned that he had extensive training in the subjects of autism and diets. We drove the five-hour car ride to see him. He was very nice, and seemed to have been in the business a long time. We were given a lot of time to explain our situation as he took notes. He helped us get Noah on the right vitamins and minerals, working around the gluten/casein free diet. Once, we had caught Noah eating dirt in the backyard. Apparently, dirt has minerals in it, and he knew his body was deprived of them. We also worked on getting some of the testing done we had learned about at the symposium. We checked urine and blood for heavy metal buildup, food allergies, candida yeast in the gut, etc. Of course, our insurance wouldn't help cover the costs of these tests, so I had to sell my favorite kidney (feel my sarcasm). We were supposed to go back home and wait the couple of weeks for the results (they had to be sent to different states), and then come back for a follow up. In the meantime, we gave Noah daily doses of mineral oil to help with the constipation.

The stomachache I had before the symposium was still there, and was said to be solved in another seven months. I was expecting our third child, but still managed to work with Noah with morning sickness and elephant-sized ankles.

The results for his testing started to roll in. Noah was officially allergic to casein, milk, grapefruit, oranges, and peanuts. I was shocked. I knew we hadn't taken him off of gluten and casein because of allergies, but because he could not digest them properly. He really did have an allergy to casein! I am so glad we started that diet. His allergy to peanuts was so low, he suggested cutting back to once or twice a month. So Noah has organic peanut butter and jelly sandwiches every once in a while. It was hard for him to give up orange juice, his favorite. We also ended up eliminating ketchup, which he had on everything. It might have been the vinegar in it. One thing I do know is that once you get gluten and casein completely out of a diet, other food allergies show up. Remember chasing a rolling ball and kicking it with the tip of your toes before you get the chance to stop it? The ball continues to roll along and you run, but never quite catch up to it. Well, that is how I felt. Once we would actually get him use to eating something that was obviously made differently than he was used to, we had to take it away.

Other tests results came in and showed a huge amount of candida yeast in his gut with zero percent healthy flora. He was also diagnosed as having Leaky Gut. Try picturing a gut with so many holes in it that it looks like a spaghetti strainer. All of the bad bodily waste escapes into the bloodstream instead of the intestines where it turns into stool, so it is floating in the blood, affecting the brain. He can eat as many healthy foods as we want, but if it isn't being absorbed, it doesn't matter. All of the healthy nutrients are flushed out. So, how do you heal the gut?

You have to get rid of the bad yeast. It is tricky, though, feeding on sugar in the body and growing in size. A lot of behavior and attention problems have been linked to candida overgrowth. You can experience headaches, constipation, severe gas and bloating, and depression. Noah did have a huge tummy. It was always bloated and hard as a rock. He never pooped. He was terrified of the toilet, pushing until he would almost pass out. Many times, he would hold it until it literally started slipping out on its own. That's a full intestine! We constantly caught him standing off to the side of the room, crossing his legs, and holding his bottom to keep it in. When he did finally go, it was *much* too big for a child. He associated the toilet time with pain and wouldn't potty train.

I was reading about an antifungal medicine that kills yeast called Nystatin. This is often used to treat thrush, as well as intestinal yeast. I really wanted to try this on Noah. We were using a little bit of liquid silver from our DAN doctor to help, but it really never worked. Noah came home from school each day in a bad mood. His stomach was hurting. His bottom was always raw and infected with yeast. Sometimes, we could even see white speckles in his stool. I am not sure if that was yeast or not, but it made sense. There were many mornings when I would wake up and go into the boys' room and see that Noah had vomited in his sleep. He would just roll over in the middle of the night and throw up over the side of his bed. There would be whole undigested pieces of food in it. I did learn that many other children with Leaky Gut have huge pieces of food in their stool. On a more positive note, by this time, Noah was starting to urinate in his little toilet.

Our daughter, Abby, was born later that winter. She was healthy and so pretty being a C-Section baby. We were not about to let them touch her with a vaccine. Noah accepted the new addition better than I expected. He did, however, leave the room screaming and holding his ears when she cried. This was normal for him. Any loud noise could set him off. A few times at school or home, he wore earphones to block out loud sounds.

On our next visit to the DAN doctor, we asked about the Nystatin pills for him. He already tested positive for yeast overgrowth, so it was obvious he needed medicine. Unfortunately, he was not an MD, so he couldn't prescribe *anything*. I had already tried the pediatrician's office, but they thought I was crazy. I succeeded once when he woke up with yeast in his mouth.

We were already watching Noah's sugar intake, but that wasn't going to be enough. We needed to starve the yeast. On the days when his sugar intake was low, he seemed more focused. His eyes looked clearer, and he never vomited. We needed to stick with a low sugar diet and get an antifungal for the yeast. So, there I was again, looking for another doctor. This time was different because I had a baby on my hip. I will spare you the details of some of the doctor visits I had with Noah while searching for help.

Chapter Seven

Nurse Hatchet's Staff

We were all sleeping soundly when we awoke to a horrible scream. I told Daniel that I would check on Noah and for him to stay in bed. I assumed he threw up again, or maybe wet the bed. When I got down the hall, I noticed the light on in the kids' bathroom. Noah was standing at the toilet, pulling on his private area screaming. I thought at first he might have been constipated. Then I realized he had to urinate. He just didn't seem to be able to. I thought that maybe his leg was asleep, or maybe he was sleepwalking. He began the ever so familiar punching of his stomach. I hollered for Dan and told him what was going on. We had him sit and try to push, but he couldn't go. We wrapped him up and took him to the Emergency Room. Noah was freaking out as they stood looking down at him. He balled his legs up and cried. They felt his abdomen and said he was impacted. As hard as it was to watch, we had to hold him down so they could try to clean some of the stool out with their fingers. They got as much stool as they could out of him and gave us a suppository to help him. Exhausted, Noah fell asleep on the way home.

 We all took a nap once home, but woke later to the same ordeal. He had to urinate, but he couldn't. We ended up back in the ER with the exact same dilemma. They cleaned some more stool out of him and gave him an enema. They inserted a catheter to relieve some urine pain. I was to follow up with the pediatrician. We went later that afternoon to see his pediatrician. He was in pain again, and still couldn't urinate. We tried several times to take him to the restroom, but it was useless. The nurses tried and tried to catheterize him, but couldn't. I had to hold him down as they kept missing. After a couple of tries, I made them stop. "Do something else!" I yelled. They sent us down to the Children's Hospital an hour away. Keep in mind that we still had to go home and get his blanket (which he never slept without), and then make the drive. His bladder was already full. Noah was so uncomfortable by the time we got there. Daniel tried to take him to potty again, while I registered him and told them a doctor was expecting us right away. Our requests were ignored as sick children (none seemed to be a life-threatening emergency) went in and out. I stopped in front of the receptionists and tapped my foot loudly. I kept on her to "Page the Doctor!"

 Finally, a couple of hours (yes, hours) later, they called Noah's name. A nurse took us back to another room where I was trying to explain that he needed to be catheterized, and she nodded, saying someone would be with us *shortly*. We waited and waited as a few more hours went by. Nobody came in. I walked around the hall looking for anyone, but no one ever came by. Noah began dancing and screaming in pain. He cried a new sound I never heard him make before. I stood up and ripped that stupid curtain back and yelled at the top of my lungs "We need a doctor now! Help us! My son needs help!" Daniel seemed embarrassed. I didn't care. At this point, Noah hadn't been able to urinate since his last catheter at the ER over twelve hours ago. A couple of nurses came flying in. I screamed at them. They told me to calm down, and I screamed some more. They catheterized him in under thirty seconds, and he filled the bag, and then another. I just stared at them in disbelief. I am not a "pain in the butt" parent, but after so many hours, they didn't take his vitals or anything. I would have waited many hours for a doctor. We just needed him catheterized. How ridiculous! They gave him a fast acting enema. I had to take him down the hall to a communal bathroom that had one toilet. The door didn't lock. I sat Noah down on the potty and knelt down in front of him. He wrapped his arms around my neck and held me close to him. He tried hard to relax when the door opened. A man was standing there and said, "Oh, excuse me." No big deal. Then about five minutes later, just as Noah seemed to have a little stool to push out of him, he walked in again. Noah started to cry because he was disrupted. I stood up and pushed the door shut and said, "Please wait and then knock, he is really sick." That jerk opened the door again and yelled at me in the hospital, "Learn to lock the door next time."

Dan walked around the corner to check on us as I was literally running out the bathroom to punch that idiot. He wouldn't let me.

The whole experience was a nightmare. My nerves

were shot, and I was having horrible chest pains. Noah never did have a bowel movement, so they admitted him. I was mad about being in that nightmare of a place, and Daniel and I were talking about transferring him to a different hospital when a very friendly nurse came down to get us and took Noah to his room. I am not saying she was an angel or anything, but when we got into the elevator exiting the ER, the lights seemed brighter and everyone glowed with sympathy for sick children. I looked at Dan and asked, "Were we just in hell?"

Many people came in to welcome us and help us fill out paper work. It was if a weight had been lifted. They made him comfortable and catheterized him once more for good. He was going to have many doctors come by in the morning, and until then, he could sleep pain free. Tears formed in my eyes as I looked down at my little boy lying in a huge metal bed. His pajamas matched all the other children's. We were there for the night.

I had a recurring nightmare shortly after Noah was diagnosed that liked to visit me late at night. I would wake up soaked, my heart pounding so hard others could hear it. We would be in a full elevator in a crowded building. It would stop to let some passengers out, and Noah got pushed with the crowd. I couldn't get past the others to grab him, and the doors would shut. Panic, nothing but pure panic. How would he tell someone who he was or who his parents were?

He ended up staying a week in the hospital. Dan and I never left together. We took turns going to get caffeine or using the restroom, afraid to leave him alone.

It is amazing how long you can function in the same clothes day after day when your child is sick. Walking down the hall with your hair sticking up in back from resting it on a hard chair seems to be the parental dress code. You nod to other parents in the hall who obviously do not want to be there either. Words didn't have to be shared. Eye contact alone was enough to satisfy your need to be outside of that building, outside of that small jail cell of a hospital room.

Later, Noah was introduced to a magical, tasteless powder called Miralax. This helped with constipation. He saw a G.I. specialist and had many X-rays and enemas, tracking his bowels. He was so impacted that stool was actually pressing on his urethra and preventing him from urinating. Noah went through a terrible ordeal trying to go. Five days later, his bowels moved enough that he could urinate by himself. We left the hospital with another G.I. appointment and a prescription for more Miralax.

We were all anxious to get back home. I remember the look Dan and I exchanged as we were told that even with insurance, his laxative would be eighty dollars a bottle. Debt is something a lot of parents of special needs children learn about. Where was Oprah when we needed her?

Back at home, we tried to go back to what we knew as "normal." Noah continued on the gluten/casein free diet, filtered water, and supplements. He was thriving in preschool, making more eye contact, and talking in two- to four-word sentences. Now, if we could only get him potty trained. I made him sit on the toilet every night and look at a book. Sometimes, he would poop for me, but he relied on medicines to help. My goal was to get his bowels trained to go on their own. I should say "one of my goals," because I had many.

Chapter Eight

BIG BOY SCHOOL

I knew that the day would come for Noah to be removed from his familiar settings of preschool and enter "Big Boy School." I guess I just didn't expect it to hit quite so fast. Sitting at an IEP (Individual Educational Plan) is never an easy thing to do, especially your first one. If your child receives any form of special services in school, you have to set one up. This is basically a meeting for parents, teachers, and therapists to sit around and talk about your child's weaknesses and strengths. I made Daniel go with me the first couple of times, and then started to handle them by myself. I usually had my invisible wall of defense up. Sometimes, I would catch myself rambling on and on, and other times, I sat and cried. Trust me, though, when I say if at any time I disagreed with anyone, I told him or her why. That is what you need to do. Who are we as parents if we do not have the ability to advocate for our children? Especially when they can't do it for themselves. Noah was to start kindergarten with a personal aide, and be with his peers as much as possible. All of his speech and occupational therapy would continue.

Big Boy School started, but it was hard for *me* to transition from a three-hour preschool program to a full day, so I can only imagine the stress on Noah. I did need the break from him though. I needed to be able to get through the grocery store without the rude comments the public seemed to give you whenever your child has a meltdown. I remember telling another parent one day, "If your child doesn't have a physical disability, meaning one that was obvious to the sight, then people automatically just think they are a brat." Unfortunately, they aren't afraid to tell you either. Sorry, but my son *does not* need a spanking! I have also noticed that the older you are, the ruder you get. My son wasn't throwing a fit because he wanted a Hot Wheel car or pack of gum. He was upset because the fluorescent lights in the store were killing his head, or the crowds were just too much and he had a sensory overload. I started to stare straight into people's eyes to make them stop looking or realize they were staring. As time went on, I realized it doesn't matter if people look at us. You don't have to explain or apologize for what your child is doing. They are people too. Worrying about what people are thinking isn't a way to live. I get a kick out of a father I met online who gives out educational business cards about autism when people are rude.

Noah was actually adjusting rather well to his new school days. He was in the main classroom with his peers sixty percent of the day. His aide stayed nearby. He left the room for speech, occupational therapy, and resource room time. The morning group time was difficult for him. Having to sit on the carpeted area of the classroom chanting dates and times annoyed him. Instead, they gave him tasks to do in the morning. He ran errands and did little stuff for the teacher. It was beneficial for everyone involved, and Noah really enjoyed getting out of the room during his hardest time.

We were given Behavior and Progress Reports daily. He seemed to enjoy emptying his backpack at night and doing his small homework assignments. The nightly schedules seemed to make our life at home easier. I have read that a lot about Autistic people. Most really need their days scheduled out for them. Sometimes, however, it can be frustrating. Running a simple errand after school instead of going straight home can throw an entire evening off. Noah likes things to be the same. That was hard for me to adjust to because I like to piddle. If I turned down a different road while driving, Noah became unsettled until he knew our schedule exactly. He had to know repeatedly where we were going.

Fall approached quickly, and Halloween was upon us. The children in the classroom celebrated with a piñata. I was again forced to realize how different my son was from others. The fits he threw having to take turns were unbearable, and I felt my defensive wall build up. I hated the other room mothers who helped with the parties. They could just smile and laugh while watching their children being children. They seemed so carefree while snapping photos and chatting. I, on the other hand, wanted it to end so that I could take my son home and get away from the lurking eyes. Eyes were *always* on us. I was sick of it. Noah looked cute in his little costume, but I avoided classroom pictures.

We made it through the rest of the year the same

way. His behavior and attitude spiked up and down. For every bad day, he had a good day later that week.

One day, I found him in his room crying because he had gotten a hold of scissors and cut huge patches of his hair. He really could have hurt himself with those, so I was thankful it was just hair. However, Noah freaked out when he saw his reflection in the mirror. He wouldn't go without his baseball cap until it grew back. He even slept in it. I had to talk the school staff into letting him wear it until his hair grew, otherwise he wouldn't go.

The kindergarten year passed quickly, and it was time for the Graduation Program. We got ready and went into the crowded gym. It was filled from one end to the other with parents, grandparents, and siblings forced to sit through the generic ceremony. We went inside and found seats. Immediately, Noah freaked out. I am not sure if it was the crowd, or just the unknowing of what was to be expected. With an entire gymnasium looking at us, we walked out with our screaming son not even five minutes later than when we arrived. I was getting used to missing things like this. I was fortunate enough to have the memories of Jared's graduation, and the hope of Abby's to come in my head. Summer was here, and the wonders of who would be his aide next year started up yet again. It seemed like there was always something to worry about.

The hot weather came. Noah took to playing Nintendo like a pro. It amazed me to see a six-year-old completing video games like he was coloring a page from a book...just ripping it out and starting with a new one. He was in love with Mario from the video games, as well as Mickey Mouse, and I started collecting things for him through EBay (another wonderful idea). He enjoyed swimming, and pretty much taught himself. One day, he just tore off his water wings and took off. We watched him learn to swim the length of the pool underwater, and dive off the diving board. It was amazing. I didn't put Noah in summer extended classes. Out here, they are in a different building with different teachers and aides. That really isn't the best situation for a child with autism. By the time he adjusted to the building and staff (if he ever did), it would be time for him to quit again. It only ran for six weeks. However, I did sign him up for speech therapy twice a week during that time, since it was with the same therapist. I really wanted to work with him at home. I did research on what therapies other parents were using. Music really seemed to stand out in my mind. I wanted to get him additional speech therapy too. I called an autism school fairly close, but they wanted thousands upon thousands of dollars in tuition. But as we all know, money does not grow on trees....but it should. Our insurance company denied Noah for this. They would, however, pay for Recovery speech therapy. It could be broken down as so: if Noah ate cheeseburgers and smoked everyday for thirty years and had a heart attack, they would pay for him to have speech therapy. They wouldn't, however, pay for a little boy with delays, someone who needed to learn language to better function in this world. That's exactly how I screamed it to them on the phone. I went to try to get financial aide for my son so I could afford his diet, his pills, and additional out-of-school therapies. We were denied, of course. I guess since we were lucky enough to have a house, we didn't qualify.

    I debated moving my family out and making a nice box under a bridge somewhere, but the summers in Missouri do get awfully hot. I had to pass on that one. Do you remember the woman from the grocery store that had half a dozen kids? Well, she would qualify. Amazing how the government works with its money. I also went to the Board for the Handicapped. They accepted Noah's application, but also denied us any financial help. I also accepted his handicap delay, however you want to say it, but we still couldn't get help. It is a crazy, messed up situation, I tell you!

I joined an Autism/Asperger Syndrome support group, and took my kids to the park where we were supposed to meet. Only two other couples showed up. We kept in touch briefly, but that fell through. I made phone calls to other parents of special needs children to try to get monthly play dates, but nobody seemed interested. I was very disappointed.

One night while surfing the web, I read that an autism research group called National Alliance for Autism Research (NAAR) was coming to St. Louis for a walk. I signed my family up. It was a few months away, but I looked forward to it. It would make me feel good collecting money for this cause, even if we barely had any. I knew people I could get to donate. We all need to donate for research.

Chapter Nine

ALL OF THE WHOOPLA

The time was coming quickly for Noah to enter the first grade. He was getting taller and losing some of that baby fat look to his face. His speech was improving, but his physical moments of depression increased. I was starting to handle the idea of him going to school in a more relaxed manner. He fit in well with the other children in his class, and they were so respectful toward him.

He was great at staying on his diet. He would ask me if certain foods had milk. I would tell him, "Yes," and ask, "What will milk do to Noah?" He always replied with, "Milk makes Noah sick, gives me tummy ache." It was easier for me to say, "Milk." I didn't know if he would understand all the different glutens, so I just say, "Has milk," about all of the foods he couldn't have. After all, he *is* allergic to milk, and so many foods are off limits.

We were still facing bowel problems and yeast build up. These caused infections around his bottom and constipation. He took the Miralax, and we slipped him some mineral oil. I was still trying to find him a better doctor. Sadly, there aren't many out there who specialize in autism. I remember a certain feeling of relief and calmness as I pushed the grocery cart through the store one day while the boys picked out items for school. Noah seemed very excited about going back as we sorted through the packs of pencils and markers. The aisle was very crowded, but he was handling it well. Nobody could tell that he had any developmental delays. "Mom, look!" he shouted, as he held up his prized Sponge Bob backpack. I smiled. "You can have it, sweetie." Deep down I knew that without his diet, he wouldn't be focusing and speaking so well. Thank God for the internet.

I got a phone call from the Special Education Department from school. They had found a new paraprofessional for Noah one week before school was to start back for the year. I went to meet her. She seemed nice enough, and I was just glad they had found someone. Starting school off with substitutes isn't the best way to go about a new year.

Daniel and I had to fight the School Board to get Noah his own aide, another attempt to cut costs somewhere. Apparently, someone in the district thought it would be okay for Noah to share a paraprofessional with another child in the room. They were wrong. Noah proved that to them in his own way. He had a tantrum and ran out the front door of the school one day, heading toward the street. He doesn't fear things like being hit by a car. Many autistic people don't. I remember picking him up from school later that day, and they were so calm, like, "By the way." I exploded with rage. I yelled at everyone. They were too calm about it, and acted like they didn't need to call me at home and tell me!

Needless to say, he was kept home from school while we again fought for his needs. I was afraid for his safety. It is amazing how a group of men from a school district can try to lecture you, and still get surprised by an advocating mother. They turned to Dan to see if he would, perhaps, make me be quiet. Not likely. I wasn't there to make friends. If you give in to the school and listen to their ramblings about cutting costs or trying this or doing that, the one who will suffer will be your child. I would call meeting after meeting and stay in their faces until they realized this mother knew the laws and wasn't going to stop. Now, Noah had his own aide for school, and a semi-sense of relief could set in. It was just sad and scary that it took what it did for them to realize this. The whole time we were fighting for him to have his own aide, he took it upon himself to show them by almost running into the street.

Once Noah started the first grade, he adjusted rather quickly. We were still having the common issues we addressed in the past, like transitioning with rooms and activities. I suggested that they put a written schedule on his desk so he had time to adjust to the changes in the days. His paraprofessional really seemed to pay close attention to his needs and his moods. She was brutally honest at times too. This took me many months to get used to and accept. Honestly, it is what we all needed. Sugar coating things just doesn't make it easier. That was a problem we had in the past with an aide. Each day, she came out smiling and telling me he had a great day. At the end of the year, as we sat in the IEP meeting, we found out all the negative problems he was having. We were blinded to those, and that wasn't right.

This year, his aide sat at a table in the corner of the room very close to his desk. That way, she would always be there when he needed her, and out of sight when he didn't. It was always important to us that Noah had the independence he deserved when he was ready. We didn't want him to go through school always expecting someone to help. We wanted to let him choose when he needed that extra help. He was spending more time in the classroom with peers and making attempts to chat with others at lunch.

I was able to pick Noah up from school, so I had close contact with the staff. This way, I could find out about Noah's days. Academically, Noah was doing wonderfully. He took to math and reading like a pro. He was obviously a very intelligent child, but masked from this fact because of the autism. I was determined to pick pieces of that
mask off of him like a puzzle, even if it took the rest of my life. Puzzles. Puzzle pieces are the symbol of the autism ribbon, because it is, in fact, a puzzling disorder.

Behavior wise, though, Noah still needed a lot of help. Daniel and I really thought that Noah was finally realizing his differences. He did seem like he was depressed a lot, and sometimes making the comment, "I wish me dead." Heartbreaking is the only word to describe this. I, too, suffered severe depression, knowing my son was starting to realize more than before. I couldn't help but think of my life as compared to other parents. My son had heartache over his differences, while other parents faced the dilemma of if their child struck out at baseball or didn't like reading at school. Noah was to receive occupational therapy once a week. We called another IEP meeting and set it up so that his paraprofessional could take him to the gym, hallway, or even the nurse's office for movement when he needed to unwind or suffered a sensory overload. They dribbled basketballs or ran in circles. Sometimes, when the noises of the other children were too much, he could go into the nurse's office and hide inside his sleeping bag, or wear a weighted pad around his shoulders.

This wasn't something we wanted him to depend on as a daily routine, but as emergencies called for it the option was there. He would be refreshed a few minutes later, and be able to return to the room when he was ready and start fresh. We all realized during an IEP meeting that having a planned time for occupational therapy wasn't the best idea. What if Noah was doing great that day, and we pulled him out for therapy when he didn't need it, and say two days later, he was overloaded with stress, but he couldn't do anything to comfort himself because it wasn't scheduled. It didn't make a bit of sense. Once or twice a week, the occupational therapist met with his paraprofessional to see how things were going. It was a super plan, and really helped him get through rough days.

Meanwhile, at home, we planned for our first official Walk for Autism. We made tee shirts and posters, and collected money from our friends and relatives. It ended up being quite an overwhelming day. They set up different bouncy rides like you would see at a carnival, and had hot dog and popcorn stands. I stood in line with my mother, waiting to turn our money in, while my dad and husband took the kids to see the fire truck on display.

A crowd was really forming around us. I saw a mother standing there with her son who obviously had autism. He was older, maybe in his late teens or early twenties. He towered over his mother in height. His hair was the exact shade of Noah's too. He seemed very happy being there. For some reason, I was drawn to look over at him, and once I did, I burst into tears. I cried so hard when I saw this young man. We always talked about Noah's future, but it seemed so far away, and of course, as his parents, we hoped for the best. I am not sure what made me lose it, most likely the fact that he looked so much like Noah, but it was obviously what I needed. Sometimes, you stay strong for so long to fight, you forget about other emotions. That is healthy too. I really wanted to be there and walk for a cure, so I didn't let a few tears stop me. The ending results were amazing as hundreds of thousands of dollars were collected for research. We planned to join again the following year.

My heart started to act up again. I found myself seeing the doctor about the anxiety attacks I was suffering from. At first, I felt stupid going there and telling them that I was passing out, but the fainting got worse. I was put on antidepressants and had to wear a heart monitor for a month in hopes that they could catch one of these episodes.

A couple weeks into the month, I had one. I woke up in the middle of the
night to a pounding heart. I recorded it and called the doctor. I sent the results over the phone like a fax. A few minutes later, my doctor called and told me to get to the hospital fast. My heart was beating two hundred and twelve beats per minute. Stress! Parents who do not have

the stress of having a child with special needs might say they do, but they don't really know our stress. It is different. We as parents feel helpless and defensive, strong and weak all at the same time. I was sent to a specialist and scheduled to have surgery done. A few weeks later, as I laid on the bed in the surgery unit of a strange hospital being prepped, a nurse leaned over so I could see her face and asked me what the tattoo on my leg meant. "It's an Autism Awareness Ribbon," I whispered, "Make sure I wake up, okay? My kids need me."

She jokingly asked me, "What do you want from the bar?"

"Something fruity, and can I have one of those cute ER doctors from NBC be my waiter?" I mumbled as I entered my induced coma.

I had super ventricular tachycardia corrected that day, in hopes of being able to stop racing heartbeats and the stress of anxiety attacks. Now bring it on! (No, not really!)

Chapter Ten

WASHINGTON D.C.

I like to think of myself as a pro on the internet. On one of my many nights of researching autism, I came across information on a huge conference being held in Washington D.C. It was a DAN conference. There were going to be many experts on autism, DAN doctors from around the world, parents, educators, and some amazing authors to share their experiences. It was also going to be very expensive. This time, I made Daniel sell *his* favorite kidney (again with the sarcasm), and we made the plans to go. My first trip on an airplane too! Daniel and I both were excited to be there. We took a quick tour the day before the conference was to start. We walked through the memorials and museums and rode the subway (wow, is that a bullet hole?), and prepared for the lectures. I had to make sure we saw the Lincoln Memorial before we went back to the hotel. I really wanted to run through the water yelling for "Forest," but I didn't think they would like that. Besides, I really didn't think Tom Hanks was in town.

The first day was a bit overwhelming, to say the least. The crowd at the conference was enormous! So many people with so much passion. This wasn't a rough, pushy crowd. Each individual there had compassion on their face, either for their child or their career. We bought at least a dozen books, tried samples of gluten free foods, stopped by booths to see what vitamins they offered, and picked out advocating hats and pins. During the lectures, we filled our notebooks. One particular speaker asked the crowd, "Whose child was developing fine until they had their MMR vaccines?"

The entire room was silent, and almost every hand went up in a room that seated thousands. Sometimes, reality is such a slap in the face. I sobbed. Music started to play, and a video started in memory of all of the little children who passed away from their vaccine. It was the most emotional moment I have ever faced with strangers in my life. It chilled me right down to the bone. Later that afternoon, the mother whose book taught me about the diet Noah was on, spoke. This was my second time hearing her speak. When she was finished, a crowd formed around her. They usually took a break between speakers. I walked up to the stage and waited patiently. She seemed very nice, listening to people and smiling. I called out her name, and when she looked at me, I told her that I wanted her to know how much her book changed our lives. Our son was doing really well with talking and making eye contact, and it was because she wrote a book, not because a doctor told us what to do, and I wanted to say thank you. She hugged me. It was a nice moment for me.

The second day was even better. We again listened and took notes. A female doctor from the next state over from us spoke. She was a DAN doctor, and gave an amazingly smart and compassionate speech. This time, I walked quickly to the stage. Daniel is rather shy, and I think he is amazed how I can talk to people I haven't met before. I pushed my way past the crowd and grabbed her arm. I asked her, "Please see my son. There isn't anyone else, and he needs help. Please take a new client." She said yes. I was beaming! A DAN doctor for Noah! That night, they held a dinner and silent auction. They had tables arranged by states, in hopes that people could share knowledge, or in my opinion, just relax for an evening of conversation with someone on the same level. You wouldn't believe how much people can say to new faces. It is different. We all know, to an extent, what the other feels and goes through. It was quite a night. Friendships formed, if even just for one night. We were all relaxed and could talk without being judged or feeling like we were.

  The third day passed quickly. I even went up to the microphone and asked a couple questions. Hey, that's why we were there. I wasn't about to go home wishing that I would have said something. A doctor was there talking about Leaky Gut. We already knew Noah had this, but he was talking about stool having big pieces of undigested food in it. I asked him if he had ever heard of a child throwing up rather large pieces of food. He had, and said, "The yeast buildup is probably very high." Healthy living flora is in every gut, and helps with the digestion process. Noah didn't have any of his left. The candida yeast in his intestines was happily multiplying within him. He would sit up several times a month in the middle of the night and lean over the side of his bed and vomit. We would never hear him because he never cried out. He would just fall back asleep, and we would find it in the morning. Whatever he had for dinner would be there, undigested. Putting your child on healthy flora is always recommended. This is called a lactobacillus. It contains live, healthy colonies for your gut. Have you ever been on a medicine from the doctor and gotten a yeast infection? Have you ever heard someone say, "Eat yogurt to help that?" Yogurt has healthy flora in it. However, if you have dairy/casein allergies, it's impossible. The first thing I was going to have our new DAN doctor do was put Noah on an antifungal. We had so much to do before we saw her. I wanted to read and write down all of my questions before I got there and forgot everything, including my name.

Before we left Washington, I called my mom and told her the information on Noah's new doctor in case the plane went down. She said I was nuts. Hey, I needed to be covered! As we sat on the plane, the man on the other side of me looked down at some of the books in my lap. He asked me if I was studying autism. I explained to him about the conference and briefly about Noah. He talked the whole flight home. He was a chiropractor who did a lot of adjustments on special needs children, and had a good list of autistic clients. Adjustments? Maybe that was something I needed to look into when I got finished with the other one million things we wanted to do. Exhausted and excited, we got home safely.

Chapter Eleven

DIETS, DETOX, AND DRUGS…OH MY!

I was very anxious about telephoning our new doctor, but disappointed when the reality of the four-week waiting period set in. It seemed like each day, Daniel and I thought of a new question to write down in our notebook of stuff to ask her. We prepared Noah with the news of our long journey to Chicago. He was so excited!

Each day, he would ask me if it was time to go, and finally, when the time did come, I packed some coloring books and snacks, and we set off. It was a very long ride, but it was what we were waiting for for many years. We made wonderful timing, and only got lost once at the end. Once there, more reality set in. I guess I expected a huge flashing light with an arrow pointing down, screaming in neon colors, "Here is the answer to autism!" Perhaps a few fireworks. Nothing too fancy, just a Vegas theme, but I was shocked to see such a small office building. We sat in the car and caught our breath.

Once inside, we had to wait a bit. Noah played with

the toys in the waiting room. The doctor was very nice and had remembered us from the conference. She did a quick exam and gently pinched his tummy, making the remark, "Ah, he is doughy," which started the nickname "Doughy Noey." We went to her office and did a complete history and set up some new tests to give her more info. She was very impressed with the choice of supplements I had him on, only adding a couple of new ones. Daniel and I were very satisfied with the amount of time and effort she gave us for that visit. Aside from the fact that her fee was more than a house payment, we left Chicago happy, knowing that he was going to get all of the minerals and vitamins he needed, and was going to get the famous methyl B12 shots everyone raved about in Washington. There was also more testing to do. She thanked us for already having him gluten and casein free and on some vitamins. She seemed very pleased to see the results we had of his stool and food allergy testing. "It is very helpful when parents are up to date with the latest findings in autism, and when they keep an open enough mind to try them," she said.

Back at home, I had to cut Noah's hair, collect stool, and get blood work for his testing. Until the results were in, we had to fill his prescription for Nystatin and the B12 shots. It's strange how you can overcome something that the very thought of makes you sick. I couldn't have ever imagined giving anyone a shot, let alone my own child. Noah had a different opinion. He wanted his mom to do it. I wanted Dan to handle that part. Noah won. I am now a nurse, among every other title mothers have.

We immediately started to see results from the Nystatin. Noah seemed to be able to go potty more and with less strain. At first, he got another yeast infection on his bottom, but it quickly went away, and some of the bloating and hardness to his stomach followed. The black circles under his eyes remained. His behavior at home and school teeter-tottered up and down. It was hard for him to express his emotions, as it always had been. Sometimes, his frustration was so overwhelming he would scream and scream. Maybe because we didn't understand what was going on inside of him, or maybe because he didn't understand why we didn't understand. We learned to read what kind of day he was going to have by the way his face looked. When Noah had deep, sunken in eyes with black underneath, we knew we were in for a bad day. The Nystatin worked on the built up yeast, but as it was working its way out, his diet would put a little back in. We had to be very careful of his sugar intake. It was as if a war was going on inside of his gut.

We had the pleasure of hearing Elaine Gottschall speak before she passed away. She is the author of the famous book entitled *Breaking the Vicious Cycle*. This describes the road to good intestinal health through the Specific Carbohydrate Diet. Many people were talking about their experiences with this diet, as well as the gluten and casein free diet. It was very impressive to hear her and read her words. Unfortunately, in Noah's case, they allowed dairy, and he is allergic to it. It does have yummy nut flour recipes that are sugar free, which Noah likes. I didn't know you could ground up nuts in a food processor and make flour!

Over the next few weeks, Noah's test results started to roll in. His stool showed a lot of yeast, and his hair and blood showed a huge amount of heavy metal buildup, anything from copper to bismuth to aluminum. He also had a lot of arsenic (scary) and mercury. We assumed mercury would be there because of the big controversy over vaccine poisoning. We were ones who believed he was fine until he got an MMR vaccine. I know doctors argue over this, but most still *only* believe what they read about in medical school. Nothing is set in stone. Besides, I dare one of them to stand up at a conference and tell ten thousand parents in an auditorium they are wrong. There are a lot of things in life that I am unsure of. I do try to keep an open mind. One thing I will take to my grave believing in is that my son was born "normal." He was developing and hitting all of his baby milestones on time, some even above average. It was after his MMR vaccine that things started going downhill. There isn't a person around, medical degree or otherwise, that will change my mind about that. So what can a person do to get rid of heavy metals from the body? Well, the medical term for it is "chelating." Chelating is a word that was new to both Daniel and I as we sat at the conference in D.C. I remember leaning over and asking someone else what it meant. This is exactly what our new DAN doctor wanted to do with Noah. To put it in simple terms, a chelating agent enters the body and binds itself to the metals, which are then eliminated from the body. You will also be asked to remove "loose" contributors to metals, like seafood or any metal cavity fillers in the mouth. If a vaccine is absolutely necessary, make sure it is thimerosal free! Ask questions and ask to see the package it comes in. This is your child.

    I did remember a little about detoxing and trying to heal the stomach from the conference, but most of it I knew we would learn as it happened. I was scared and anxious to get started. Detoxing is a very frightening word. It makes me think of an old rock star trying to clean up. Before we could even start, we had to have a blood test done to check liver and kidney functions. This test is repeated every couple of months. Noah really was getting better at having his blood drawn. It used to take two of us to hold him down. We get in with the same tech each time, which seems to make him more comfortable.

We started Noah out on a Glutathione lotion and TD-DMPS (Transdermal DMPS is a chelating agent) that has a nasty skunk smell. You do get used to it though. It sort of reminds me of that rotten egg or home perm hair smell. Did I mention that it stinks? I also took it upon myself to put him on a detoxing aide capsule from Kirkman's Lab. The first few months of detoxing were rough. He looked terrible in the eyes and was very anxious and crabby. When a good day did come, he would be very verbal and show his personality, which over the years has proven to be very silly like mine. With each good day came hope.

Depression, screaming, "I hate you," and foul language followed a bad day. His doctor told us these moods were fairly normal. He had a lot going on inside of him.

The results of the blood and fecal tests done every two to three months showed very slow movements of heavy metals being excreted from Noah's body. They were moving in the direction we wanted them to, but it was going to be a long road. I was always adjusting his vitamins and minerals after retesting his blood.

Noah started second grade with the same paraprofessional he had in the first grade. They were good friends, and I felt comfortable knowing she was working with him. Academically, Noah flourished. He read and did math problems without having to think twice. He has problems with winning and losing, and we are still working on this. The resource room teacher made it a point to have other students work with Noah on playing board games during free time.

The time was drawing near for the second autism walk. I was trying to think of a way to get Noah's school involved. I had been at the pharmacy earlier that day where they were selling paper shoes that you could hang on the wall in the store. The money collected from the shoes was going toward juvenile diabetes. So I had my brother-in-law print out enough paper footprints for the entire school. I wrote a letter introducing Noah and briefly telling about autism. I invited everyone from the school to "join in" on the walk by buying a footprint for a dollar and then taping it up in the gym. Each footprint was put in front of the other so they were in a walking pattern. This was a great way for the students to be introduced to autism, and an even better way to collect money for research. If a student donated more than one dollar, they got stickers for their footprints. I gave the class that donated the most a cupcake party. The Student Council helped each morning by collecting the money and keeping track of which teachers they had. It turned out to be a good idea. I noticed that more students acknowledged Noah's presence in the hallway and attempted to make conversations with him. This was another way for him to stop and take time to make eye contact and practice his cognitive skills.

At home, Noah was really joining in on playing with the neighbors and friends Jared invited over. He was laughing and taking turns. It was amazing to see. Jared's friends treated Noah with respect and just accepted him as another kid to play with. That's all we really wanted.

When Christmas time came close, I was asked to sign a permission form giving the thumbs up for Noah to join his classmates in the music concert at school. I was against this because of my own fears of my son freaking out and being stared at, but both his paraprofessional and his resource room teacher informed me that he had worked hard and should be given a chance to join in. On the night of the concert, my family and I sat patiently waiting and wondering what would happen. I was so nervous it made me sick. The second graders came out onto the risers wearing Santa hats and sunglasses. Noah was so calm and collected. They sang Christmas songs and did generic hand gestures in rhythm to the music. When it was time for solos, I watched Noah take the microphone and sing a couple of lines by himself. Tears rolled down my cheeks as I sat in awe. What a moment that was. Daniel and I laid in bed that night talking about the music program, and how it was the best thing we have ever witnessed. It took Noah over two years to actually stay in the room during music class. Quite a Christmas gift!

Noah continued to do well academically for the remaining part of the second grade. He seemed to be making more of an effort socially too. He even got invited to a couple of birthday parties.

I was seeing a chiropractor for my lower back pain for a while when I ran into a mother of a child Noah had went to preschool with. Her son had some different issues and had been receiving cranial adjustments. She explained to me how well he was doing after each adjustment. His behavior and attention in school improved and returned a few days prior to his next adjustment. It reminded me of the chiropractor who made conversation with me on the airplane. My mind had been so preoccupied with everything else, I forgot to research that.

I talked briefly to my chiropractor, and we made Noah an appointment. After school one day, I took Noah in and he laid on the table, tummy down. It was basically like a gentle massage on the back of his head. There weren't any quick movements. The adjustment didn't take long, and Noah did wonderfully.

The next day, I was met at the doorway of Noah's school. He had a terrible day! It consisted of screaming, crying, and cussing. He didn't look good. This went on with every adjustment, and gradually got worse. I finally made the decision to stop taking him. I believe each and every parent that says they have good results. This just wasn't helping Noah.

Toward the end of the year, Dan and I rented a cabin for the weekend close to Branson. It was nice to take the kids on a little trip. Noah was a lot of fun while we went through crazy museums and played board games as a family back at the cabin. We like to do things like that. It is really important to me that my children stay close. I hope with all of my heart that Jared and Abby choose to be in Noah's life as adults.

Noah graduated the second grade on the honor roll, and we set out to have a wonderful summer.

Chapter Twelve

SET NOTHING IN STONE

A handful of days before Noah was to start the third grade, I got a phone call from the School District. The paraprofessional that had worked so well and accomplished so much with Noah over the last two years was moving out of state. Normally, news like that would have made me snap, but Dan reminded me that the only ones Noah could always depend on for being there was us. Besides, it wouldn't be healthy for him to depend so much on just one person. They had another paraprofessional lined up who had lots of experience, and things worked out just fine.

Just like the quick changes of his paraprofessional, the future for Noah could change in the blink of an eye. His progress and what he will be able to achieve will never be set in stone. Each time we have his blood work taken to check his detoxing levels, it comes back slightly different. As the school years change, the class work gets more difficult. Noah always seems ready for the new challenges.

A particular average day will pass and he will do or say something amazing, which always seems to remind me of that day in the doctor's office waiting for a diagnosis. At that time in my life, the future seemed doomed. I wanted to crawl under a rock and die.

Over time, I accepted what has happened and found my own way to try to make a difference. Yes, I would like to be one of those parents writing in, claiming their child no longer has a diagnosis of autism on their medical records, but I don't know if that's in the cards for us. It took the doctors too long to help us find out what was wrong. We lost a lot of valuable time. I do know that if it wasn't for other parents writing their experiences down, I might not have been able to experiment with alternative treatments. I hope that one day more physicians take the time to research and practice them in their offices. The DAN doctor list is way too short. Perhaps Noah's story will encourage both parents and doctors to come forward and make a difference in the life of a special needs child.

As time continues to move forward, I pray for Noah's life to be easier for him. I also hope that more parents will take the time to investigate possible alternatives in treatment for their special needs child. I think about the argument I just had, not two weeks ago, at Abby's four-year checkup. That doctor shook her had at me over why Abby wasn't vaccinated. Maybe one day it will be less of an ordeal when alternative medical decisions are made. In the mean time, I stay strong. I remember why I am making the decisions I do when I look into Noah's eyes.

I cannot end my book with all of the stories of Noah's teen and adult years, because he is still a child. I'm just going to make sure it has a "happily ever after" in it somewhere. He *has* come such a long way over the years since he was diagnosed. It is because of all the things we tried on our own.

    I want to leave you with my favorite poem, given to me by another mother of a special needs child when I was down in the dumps. Keep faith, and remember, for every bad day, a good will soon follow.

Epilogue

WELCOME TO HOLLAND
By Emily Perl Kingsley

I am often asked to describe the experience of raising a child with a disability to try to help people who have not shared that unique experience to understand it, to imagine how it would feel. It's like this…

When you're going to have a baby, it's like planning a fabulous vacation trip to Italy. You buy a bunch of guidebooks and make your wonderful plans. The Coliseum. The Michelangelo David. The gondolas in Venice. You may learn some handy phrases in Italian. It's all very exciting.

After months of eager anticipation, the day finally arrives. You pack your bags, and off you go. Several hours later, the plane lands. The stewardess comes in and says, "Welcome to Holland."

"Holland?!" you say. "What do you mean Holland? I signed up for Italy! I'm supposed to be in Italy. All my life I've dreamed of going to Italy."

But there's been a change in the flight plan. They've landed in Holland, and there you must stay.

The important thing is that they haven't taken you to a horrible, disgusting, filthy place, full of pestilence, famine, and disease. It's just a different place.

So you must go out and buy new guidebooks. And you must learn a whole new language. And you will meet a whole new group of people you would never have met.

It's just a different place. It's slower-paced than Italy, less flashy than Italy. But after you've been there for a while and you catch your breath, you look around... and you begin to notice that Holland has windmills...and Holland has tulips. Holland even has Rembrandts.

But everyone you know is busy coming and going from Italy...and they're all bragging about what a wonderful time they had there. And for the rest of your life, you will say "Yes, that's where I was supposed to go. That's what I had planned."

And the pain of that will never, ever, ever, ever go away...because the loss of that dream is a very very significant loss.

But...if you spend your life mourning the fact that you didn't get to Italy, you may never be free to enjoy the very special, the very lovely things...about Holland.

Helpful Links

Listed below are helpful internet links I have or still do use on our journey.

ANDI (Autism Network for Dietary Intervention)
www.autismndi.com
The Autism Diet
www.autism-diet.com
The Autism Research Institute
www.autismwebsite.com
Autism Society of America
www.autism-society.org
Autism Today
www.autismtoday.com
Autism Web
www.autismweb.com
Chocolate Emporium
www.choclat.com
1-888-choclat
Cure Autism Now (CAN)
www.cureautismnow.org

Energy Foods
www.ener-g.com
Families for Early Autism Treatment
www.feat.org
Feingold Program
www.feingold.org
1-800-321-3287
The Gluten/Casein Free Diet
www.gfcfdiet.com
Gluten Free Pantry
www.glutenfreepantry.com
Kirkmans
www.kirkmanlabs.com
1-800-245-8282
NAAR
(National Alliance for Autism Research)
www.naar.org
National Vaccine Info Center
www.909shot.com
PECS
(picture exchange communications system)
www.pecs.com
1-888-732-7462

Tate Publishing & *Enterprises*

Tate Publishing is committed to excellence in the publishing industry. Our staff of highly trained professionals, including editors, graphic designers, and marketing personnel, work together to produce the very finest books available. The company reflects the philosophy established by the founders, based on Psalms 68:11,

"THE LORD GAVE THE WORD AND GREAT WAS THE COMPANY OF THOSE WHO PUBLISHED IT."

If you would like further information, please call
1.888.361.9473
or visit our website
www.tatepublishing.com

TATE PUBLISHING & *Enterprises*, LLC
127 E. Trade Center Terrace
Mustang, Oklahoma 73064 USA